Fiddlin' For Fun Functionally

by Patty Nicholas

Teachers Book

Design: Aean Pinheiro

© Distributed Exclusively by
Alfred Publishing Co., Inc.

ISBN 0-87487-680-X

INTRODUCTION

After 15 years of playing in Orchestras ranging from Youth Symphonies to University Orchestras I found myself in western Kansas in a community that had a one-performance-a-year volunteer orchestra. After they played the Messiah in the spring they wouldn't play again 'till the next spring. Well, I was lonesome for musical outlets so I put an ad in the paper to teach violin, viola, guitar or voice. The only response I received was from a flat picking bluegrass guitarist who asked if I could fiddle. I responded with, "I've never tried it but if I can use my violin I'll try." I attended a rehearsal only to find a group of non-reading, bluegrass musicians and I couldn't fiddle. I couldn't hear a piece and play along. They were very patient and eager to have a fiddle player so I learned three tunes from a book.

I went to my first local fiddle contest. It was so memorable! Every contestant appeared to be 65 or older by the gray hair and I was one of only two women competing. When I signed in for the contest the old men saw me and were very encouraging. One said, "Now don't be afraid and just play right up to the mic." Others spoke of how they were glad to see a youngster join in, however, when I was through their attitude changed. "You paid money to learn how to do that," they commented. "It ain't a fiddle if there ain't no rosin on the box," and "I bet you know how to read those little dots on the page, too." Even though I took third place I knew I wasn't a fiddler and in the five years to follow I tackled the problem with intense interest.

I attended fiddle contests, studied with fiddlers, bought books, transcribed records, and played in country bands. One day I found myself teaching and playing in Tulsa, Oklahoma, where I landed a playing job in a bluegrass musical for the Gaslight Dinner Theater. The production was "The Robber Bride Groom." This was a Broadway musical written from the novel of the same name by Eudora Welty. It all came together for me.

Eudora Welty was my mother's doctoral dissertation subject. My mother loved American humorists and my father had a Doctorate in music. I was a product of my parent's interests. Even though it pained my father to see me branch off from classical music he had to accept my fiddling as a form of light-hearted music. Just as American humorists are a form of light-hearted literature. I've always enjoyed playing both fiddle in the bands and viola in the orchestras and quartets around Tulsa. I can't thank my parents enough for giving me the tools and heritage to have such a love for my music and fiddling.

Dedicated to my parents,
Dad, Millard Laing, for teaching me to appreciate the classics
and for paying for all those music lessons
and to
Mom, Nita Laing, for teaching me to appreciate folklore.
She read me the best short stories.

Contents

About Dynamics

There are no dynamic markings in this book so that you can interpret your own. Fast tunes are usually loud and Waltzes are combinations of many dynamics. When accompanying, play so that the melody can be heard. Think for yourself what would be the best dynamic. Trust your instincts and run with it!

1. Irish Washerwoman
accompaniment

students play the G,
C and D chords

traditional

For practice holding the violin try playing the first half of Irish Washerwoman with your left hand on your right shoulder. The students' book has no first and second endings. To keep their part simple they have only a repeat sign.

2. Irish Washerwoman

a look at just the chords

This is exactly the same music as number one only the student must know how to play each chord by its' name.

3. Boil 'em Cabbage Down
first version

traditional

The first two measures are a lead-in and are not numbered with the rest of the measures. Instead they are marked 'a' and 'b'. In this book the lead-ins will not be included with the numbering of the measures. Lead-ins are interchangeable and can be more than two measures.

4. Boil 'em Cabbage Down
blue jello rhythm

The 'blue jello' rhythm is another way of having the students feel the rhythm 'quarter-eighth-eighth'. These are the words commonly used in the book No 'H' in Snake. This bowing is commonly called the "Nashville Shuffle.'

5. Rubber Dolly
first version

traditional

6. Practicing the duple bowing

Practice with your left hand on your right shoulder.
Start slow and gradually accelerando.

7. Boil 'em Cabbage Down

duple variation

In measure one the student needs a good left hand position in order to hold the 2nd finger down while playing the open E. This open E is a drone note taken from the bagpipe sound.

8. Boil 'em Cabbage Down
with double stops

Watch for a good left hand position to help hold the notes on the A string while playing the open E string.

9. Tag in A

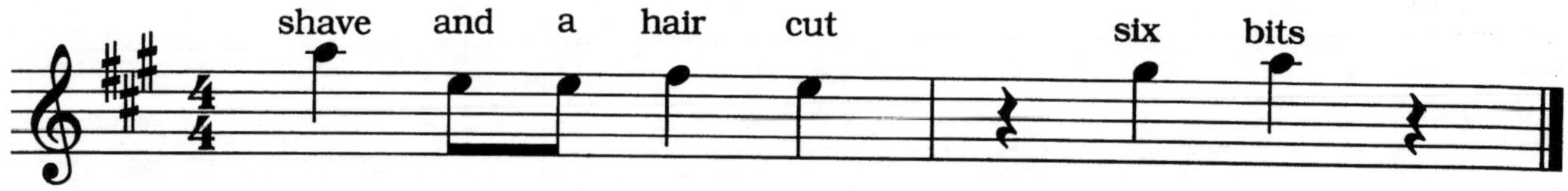

10. Boil 'em Cabbage Down
arrangement

The lead-in and the tag are separated by double bars since they are interchangeable parts. They are not numbered in with the measure numbers but are lettered 'a' and 'b'.

11. Boil 'em Cabbage Down

accompaniment

Students learn the chords in their simplest form.

12. Boil 'em Cabbage Down
just the chords

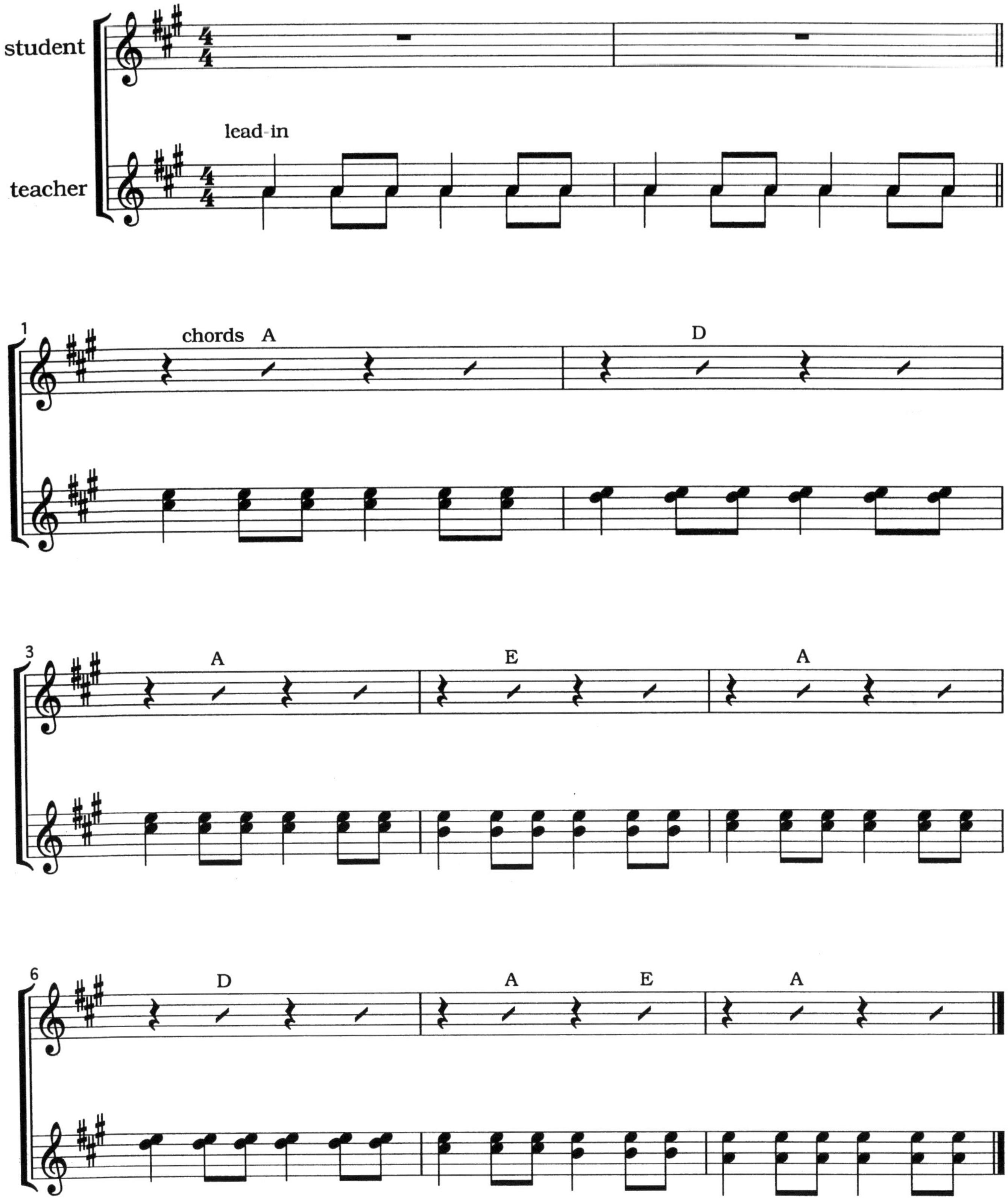

This uses the same notes as selection 11 only the student think chord names instead of notes.

13. Old Joe Clark

The line in the melody in measure 12 is a smear symbol meaning to approach the note from below

traditional

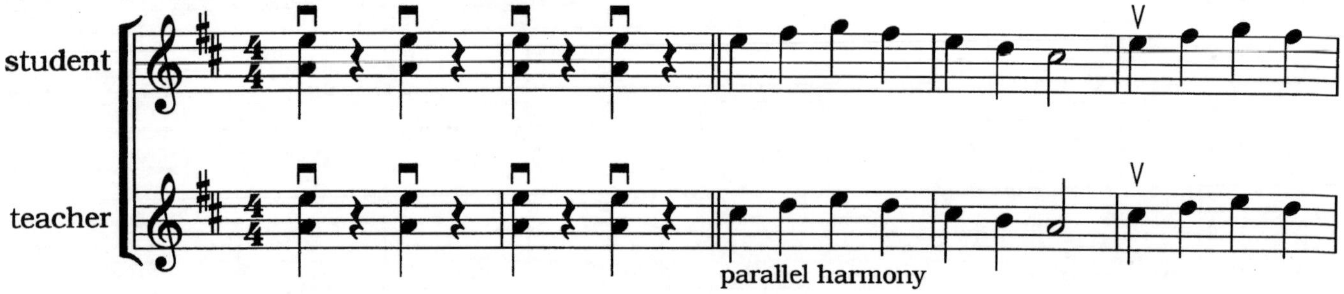

A new lead-in. The line in measure 12 is a smear and means to approach the note from below. Place the finger in the b flat position and smear it up to b natural. This is one very basic difference between playing the violin and the fiddle. Kato Havas advocates smearing when learning to find pitch. Here we incorporate it as a nuance.

14. Old Joe Clark

accompaniment

The student's new tag is based on the A chord. This selection is in the key of A mixolydian. Mixolydian mode is an A major scale with a minor seventh degree, g natural, commonly used in old English reels and modern tunes such as Rocky Top. Rocky Top and Old Joe Clark use the A and G chords for more mixolydian flavor.

15. Before Breakfast

traditional

The original name of this selection is Whiskey Before Breakfast.

16. Old Joe Clark
advanced

The rhythm in measure 12 can be felt with the jazz phrase 'here come da judge'.

17. Old Joe Clark
arrangement

A good solo arrangement for a student

verse two
tag

18. Old Joe Clark

group arrangement

When playing in a group the students can 'pass off ' the melody and accompany each other.

The students play independently in two groups.
When the student plays the melody it is called 'taking a ride'.

19. Rubber Dolly
accompaniment

An exercise in listening to chord changes while previewing a new selection.

20. Slurring

21. Rubber Dolly

advanced variation

Students who cannot play slurs yet can play just the written half notes through measure 16, then they can shuffle (blue jello) the written notes without the string crossings to the end. Students may preview by first playing the written half notes while the teacher plays the slurred notes.

22. Goofus

swing rhythm
+ means left hand pizzicato

traditional

Swing rhythm means to play eighth notes with a triplet feeling,
It should not be played too perfectly but with a loose feeling. In professional circles classical violinists are well known for not having the loose swing feel.

23. Cindy

traditional

More slurring exercise.

24. Fiddlin' Around

swing rhythm

traditional

This selection changes key every two measures. It starts in A changes to D, then G and ends in C. Instead of calling this playing through the circle of fifths a fiddler would call this playing "'round the horn".

25. Fiddlin' Around

back-up

swing rhythm

26. Amazing Grace

Swing rhythm or straight rhythm.
In the second verse (measure 17) triplets are added as an ornament.

gospel

This tune can be played with swing rhythm or straight. The triplets are an extension of the swing feel, 'just filling in the gaps' so to speak. They change the feel to

27. Boil 'em Cabbage Down

cajun style and rockin' the bow style

Cajun style means to approach the melody note from below and 'hammer on' the melody note by hammering down your finger. 'Hammer on' is a term for the same effect used with guitar chords.

28. Tags in A

29. Rubber Dolly
with double stops

In measures 5 and 13 smear into the unison.

Measure 5 and 6 should be played with the 4th finger down creating a drone note 'E'. This drone note is very common to certain types of fiddle tunes such as <u>Sally Goodin</u> . This is a good tune to try this technique on. If it is too hard the student can easily omit the open E string. Measures 5 and 13 have a double stop E unison with a smear. This is a fiddle technique that is very hard to notate. Smearing into a unison like this separates the real fiddle players from violinists. For smearing practice see selection 13, Old Joe Clark.

30. Boil 'em Cabbage Down

more accompaniment

The teacher's bowing style changes from the old fashioned "Nashville shuffle" to the Texas swing style "backstroke" bowing. The "backstroke" gets its' name from the quick down bow in measures 5 and 6.

31. Boil 'em Cabbage Down
making your own arrangement

Think of all the ways you can play Boil 'em Cabbage Down then make your own variation from the example started below. Don't forget to play a lead-in and a tag.

32. Rubber Dolly

arrangement

This is a collection of all the Rubber Dolly selections in the book.

18
22
26
30
35

39
43
47
52
56

60
64
68
72
76

33. 34. and 35. Boil 'em Cabbage Down
playing in a group

Each part plays the melody one at a time. Taking turns like this is called 'passing off' the melody.

When playing in a group each musician can play back-up (accompaniment) till their turn to take a ride (play the melody).

12
16
get ready
20
25

36. and 37. Liberty
a traditional duet

18
23
27
32
37

38. Westphalia Waltz

traditional

33
3
39
46
53
58

39. Old Joe Clark
fancy variation

8
A
11
A
G
A
14
A
G
16
A
tag
18
tag

40. Fiddlin' Around

advanced

swing rhythm
students can accompany with the chords listed in selection 25 or with the notes in selection 41.

13
G
C
17
A
D
21
G
C
25
A
D
29
G
C

41. Fiddlin' Around
more back-up

swing rhythm

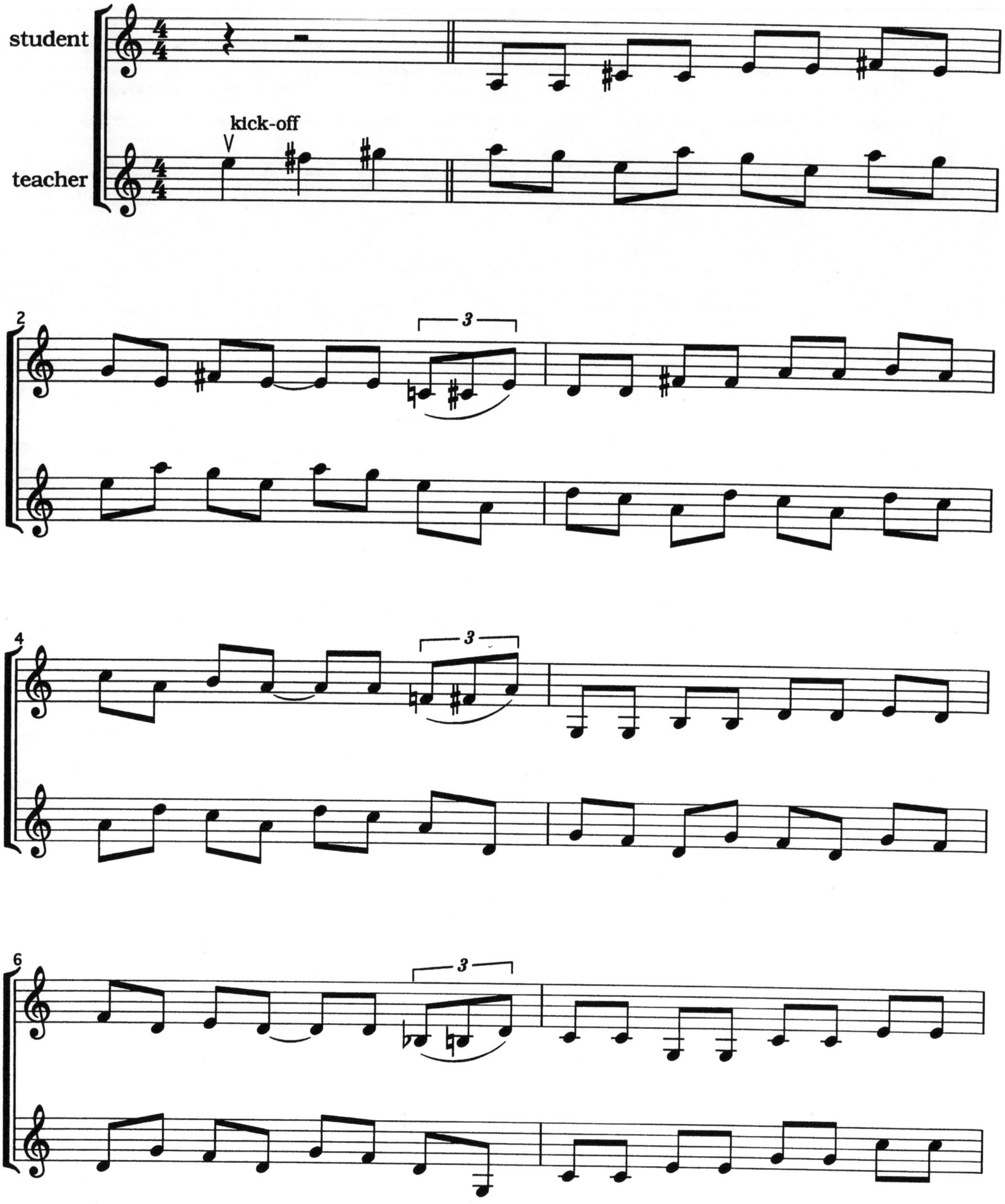

GLOSSARY

Backstroke - a bowing style common to Texas swing style. Very popular in contest fiddling. When playing running eighth notes slur three up and one down. The bow length compensation causes the down bow to be louder or a "back stroke". See selection 30 Boil 'em Cabbage Down, more accompaniment.

Cajun - see 'hammer-on'

Hammer-on - a bowing and fingering style native to Cajun music. Bowing with the Nashville shuffle you slur into the melody note. This is widley used with guitar chords also. See selection 27 Boil 'em Cabbage Down, cajun style and rockin' the bow.

Kick-off - a lead-in or introduction to a tune. Often shorter than a measure. See selection 24 Fiddlin' Around.

Lead-in - a fiddler's term for introduction. The lead-in tells the group what tempo and key the tune will be in without saying a word. Introduced in selection 3 Boil 'em Cabbage Down, first version - the first two measures are a lead-in and are not numbered with the rest of the measures. Instead they are marked 'a' and 'b'. Lead-ins are interchangeable and can be more than two measures.

Mixolydian mode - a major scale with a minor seventh degree. Tunes with this mode also use the flatted VII chord where you would expect to hear the V chord. In the key of A the I and flat VII chords are A and G just as with Old Joe Clark. This modal flavor is popular today and is in many modern American tunes such as Rocky Top. See selection 14 Old Joe Clark, accompaniment.

Nashville shuffle - a common bowing in fiddling. The same bowing is used early in the Suzuki Violin method with the Twinkle variation c. In this book it is referred to as the "blue jello" rhythm from the theory method No-H-In-Snake by Michicko Yurko. See selection 4 Boil 'em Cabbage Down, blue jello rhythm.

Pass off - in this context means to turn the melody over to another musician. See selection 18 Old Joe Clark, group arrangement and selection 33 Boil 'em Cabbage Down, playing in a group.

'Round the horn - to go around the circle of fifths with the chord changes. See selection 24 Fiddlin' Around.

Smear - to slide into the pitch from below; selection 13 Old Joe Clark. In selection 29 Rubber Dolly is a smear into a unison with the open E string. Smearing done well can make the difference between a fiddler and a violinist. Playing out of tune for the trained violinists can sometimes be so difficult that smearing can not be out of tune enough to sound right to a fiddler. Duration of the smear is important. Listening to popular music helps assimilate the feel. When playing the unison E in selection 29 the unison shouldn't be too perfect. It should be out of tune enough to hear the chorus effect.

Swing - a rhythm meaning to play ♫ like ♩♪ (triplet 3). Writing the music in 12/8 would be close but too exact. The true fiddler plays the swing feel like a loose 4/4 rhythm. The faster the fiddler swings eighth notes the more even or duple the rhythm becomes. Selection 22 Goofus.

Tag - ending or coda to a tune. First introduced in selection 9 Tag in A. Selection 10 Boil 'em Cabbage Down, arrangement - first uses a tag and explains that like the lead-in, they are variable in length and are not numbered in with the verse of the tune. In an ensemble of three lead players each should take a tag.

Taking a ride - having a turn at the melody in an ensemble. Selection 18 Old Joe Clark, group arrangement.